PERSONAL PAGE

NAME: _____

CONTACT: _____

DATE: DATE'S NAME:

WHEN: EXCITEMENT LEVEL:

WHERE:

What do you want out of the date?

What do you want to know about them?

What do you want them to know about you?

Date Fun Silliness Checklist

BATHROOM BREAK COUNT		DRINKS COUNT		TIMES CHECKED PHONE COUNT	
ME	THEM	ME	THEM	ME	THEM

♥ SUMMARY  F THE DATE

What where the highlights of the date?

Things you have in common with them?

What do you like about them?

Things that concerns/worries you about them?

Overall feeling of the date?

Would you see them again?

DATE: DATE'S NAME:

WHEN: EXCITEMENT LEVEL:

WHERE:

What do you want out of the date?

What do you want to know about them?

What do you want them to know about you?

Date Fun Silliness Checklist

BATHROOM BREAK COUNT		DRINKS COUNT		TIMES CHECKED PHONE COUNT	
ME	THEM	ME	THEM	ME	THEM

♥ SUMMARY F THE DATE

What where the highlights of the date?

Things you have in common with them?

What do you like about them?

Things that concerns/worries you about them?

Overall feeling of the date?

Would you see them again?

DATE:

DATE'S NAME:

WHEN:

EXCITEMENT LEVEL:

WHERE:

What do you want out of the date?

What do you want to know about them?

What do you want them to know about you?

🥂🎳💐 ˙◡˙ **Date Fun Silliness Checklist** ˙◡˙ 💐🎳🥂

BATHROOM BREAK COUNT		DRINKS COUNT		TIMES CHECKED PHONE COUNT	
ME	THEM	ME	THEM	ME	THEM

♥ SUMMARY 🔥F THE DATE

What where the highlights of the date?

Things you have in common with them?

What do you like about them?

Things that concerns/worries you about them?

Overall feeling of the date?

Would you see them again?

DATE:

DATE'S NAME:

WHEN:

EXCITEMENT LEVEL:

WHERE:

What do you want out of the date?

What do you want to know about them?

What do you want them to know about you?

Date Fun Silliness Checklist

BATHROOM BREAK COUNT		DRINKS COUNT		TIMES CHECKED PHONE COUNT	
ME	THEM	ME	THEM	ME	THEM

♥ SUMMARY ⬆F THE DATE

What where the highlights of the date?

Things you have in common with them?

What do you like about them?

Things that concerns/worries you about them?

Overall feeling of the date?

Would you see them again?

DATE: DATE'S NAME:

WHEN: EXCITEMENT LEVEL:

WHERE:

What do you want out of the date?

What do you want to know about them?

What do you want them to know about you?

Date Fun Silliness Checklist

BATHROOM BREAK COUNT		DRINKS COUNT		TIMES CHECKED PHONE COUNT	
ME	THEM	ME	THEM	ME	THEM

♥ SUMMARY F THE DATE

What where the highlights of the date?

Things you have in common with them?

What do you like about them?

Things that concerns/worries you about them?

Overall feeling of the date?

Would you see them again?

DATE: _____ DATE'S NAME: _____

WHEN: _____ EXCITEMENT LEVEL: _____

WHERE: _____

What do you want out of the date?

....
....
....
....

What do you want to know about them?

....
....
....
....

What do you want them to know about you?

....
....
....
....

Date Fun Silliness Checklist

BATHROOM BREAK COUNT		DRINKS COUNT		TIMES CHECKED PHONE COUNT	
ME	THEM	ME	THEM	ME	THEM

♥ SUMMARY F THE DATE

What where the highlights of the date?

....

....

....

Things you have in common with them?

....

....

....

What do you like about them?

....

....

....

Things that concerns/worries you about them?

....

....

....

Overall feeling of the date?

....

....

....

Would you see them again?

....

....

....

DATE: DATE'S NAME:

WHEN: EXCITEMENT LEVEL:

WHERE:

What do you want out of the date?

What do you want to know about them?

What do you want them to know about you?

Date Fun Silliness Checklist

BATHROOM BREAK COUNT		DRINKS COUNT		TIMES CHECKED PHONE COUNT	
ME	THEM	ME	THEM	ME	THEM

♥ SUMMARY  OF THE DATE

What where the highlights of the date?

Things you have in common with them?

What do you like about them?

Things that concerns/worries you about them?

Overall feeling of the date?

Would you see them again?

DATE: DATE'S NAME:

WHEN: EXCITEMENT LEVEL:

WHERE:

What do you want out of the date?

What do you want to know about them?

What do you want them to know about you?

Date Fun Silliness Checklist

BATHROOM BREAK COUNT		DRINKS COUNT		TIMES CHECKED PHONE COUNT	
ME	THEM	ME	THEM	ME	THEM

 SUMMARY OF THE DATE

What where the highlights of the date?

Things you have in common with them?

What do you like about them?

Things that concerns/worries you about them?

Overall feeling of the date?

Would you see them again?

DATE: DATE'S NAME:

WHEN: EXCITEMENT LEVEL:

WHERE:

What do you want out of the date?

What do you want to know about them?

What do you want them to know about you?

Date Fun Silliness Checklist

BATHROOM BREAK COUNT		DRINKS COUNT		TIMES CHECKED PHONE COUNT	
ME	THEM	ME	THEM	ME	THEM

💔 SUMMARY 🔥F THE DATE

What where the highlights of the date?

Things you have in common with them?

What do you like about them?

Things that concerns/worries you about them?

Overall feeling of the date?

Would you see them again?

DATE:

DATE'S NAME:

WHEN:

EXCITEMENT LEVEL:

WHERE:

What do you want out of the date?

What do you want to know about them?

What do you want them to know about you?

Date Fun Silliness Checklist

BATHROOM BREAK COUNT		DRINKS COUNT		TIMES CHECKED PHONE COUNT	
ME	THEM	ME	THEM	ME	THEM

💔 SUMMARY 🔥F THE DATE

What where the highlights of the date?

Things you have in common with them?

What do you like about them?

Things that concerns/worries you about them?

Overall feeling of the date?

Would you see them again?

DATE: DATE'S NAME:

WHEN: EXCITEMENT LEVEL:

WHERE:

What do you want out of the date?

What do you want to know about them?

What do you want them to know about you?

🥂🎳🎉 😄 **Date Fun Silliness Checklist** 😄 🎉🎳🥂

BATHROOM BREAK COUNT		DRINKS COUNT		TIMES CHECKED PHONE COUNT	
ME	THEM	ME	THEM	ME	THEM

♥ SUMMARY 🔥F THE DATE

What where the highlights of the date?

Things you have in common with them?

What do you like about them?

Things that concerns/worries you about them?

Overall feeling of the date?

Would you see them again?

DATE: DATE'S NAME:

WHEN: EXCITEMENT LEVEL:

WHERE:

What do you want out of the date?

What do you want to know about them?

What do you want them to know about you?

Date Fun Silliness Checklist

BATHROOM BREAK COUNT		DRINKS COUNT		TIMES CHECKED PHONE COUNT	
ME	THEM	ME	THEM	ME	THEM

♥ SUMMARY 🔥F THE DATE

What where the highlights of the date?

Things you have in common with them?

What do you like about them?

Things that concerns/worries you about them?

Overall feeling of the date?

Would you see them again?

DATE: DATE'S NAME:

WHEN: EXCITEMENT LEVEL:

WHERE:

What do you want out of the date?

What do you want to know about them?

What do you want them to know about you?

Date Fun Silliness Checklist

BATHROOM BREAK COUNT		DRINKS COUNT		TIMES CHECKED PHONE COUNT	
ME	THEM	ME	THEM	ME	THEM

❤ SUMMARY F THE DATE

What where the highlights of the date?

Things you have in common with them?

What do you like about them?

Things that concerns/worries you about them?

Overall feeling of the date?

Would you see them again?

DATE: DATE'S NAME:

WHEN: EXCITEMENT LEVEL:

WHERE:

What do you want out of the date?

What do you want to know about them?

What do you want them to know about you?

Date Fun Silliness Checklist

BATHROOM BREAK COUNT		DRINKS COUNT		TIMES CHECKED PHONE COUNT	
ME	THEM	ME	THEM	ME	THEM

♥ SUMMARY ♨F THE DATE

What where the highlights of the date?

Things you have in common with them?

What do you like about them?

Things that concerns/worries you about them?

Overall feeling of the date?

Would you see them again?

DATE:

DATE'S NAME:

WHEN:

EXCITEMENT LEVEL:

WHERE:

What do you want out of the date?

What do you want to know about them?

What do you want them to know about you?

🥂🎳💐 ·–· **Date Fun Silliness Checklist** ·–· 💐🎳🥂

BATHROOM BREAK COUNT		DRINKS COUNT		TIMES CHECKED PHONE COUNT	
ME	THEM	ME	THEM	ME	THEM

♥ SUMMARY F THE DATE

What where the highlights of the date?

Things you have in common with them?

What do you like about them?

Things that concerns/worries you about them?

Overall feeling of the date?

Would you see them again?

DATE: DATE'S NAME:

WHEN: EXCITEMENT LEVEL:

WHERE:

What do you want out of the date?

What do you want to know about them?

What do you want them to know about you?

Date Fun Silliness Checklist

BATHROOM BREAK COUNT		DRINKS COUNT		TIMES CHECKED PHONE COUNT	
ME	THEM	ME	THEM	ME	THEM

♥ SUMMARY 🔥F THE DATE

What where the highlights of the date?

Things you have in common with them?

What do you like about them?

Things that concerns/worries you about them?

Overall feeling of the date?

Would you see them again?

DATE:

DATE'S NAME:

WHEN:

EXCITEMENT LEVEL:

WHERE:

What do you want out of the date?

What do you want to know about them?

What do you want them to know about you?

Date Fun Silliness Checklist

BATHROOM BREAK COUNT		DRINKS COUNT		TIMES CHECKED PHONE COUNT	
ME	THEM	ME	THEM	ME	THEM

 SUMMARY OF THE DATE

What where the highlights of the date?

Things you have in common with them?

What do you like about them?

Things that concerns/worries you about them?

Overall feeling of the date?

Would you see them again?

DATE:

DATE'S NAME:

WHEN:

EXCITEMENT LEVEL:

WHERE:

What do you want out of the date?

What do you want to know about them?

What do you want them to know about you?

Date Fun Silliness Checklist

BATHROOM BREAK COUNT		DRINKS COUNT		TIMES CHECKED PHONE COUNT	
ME	THEM	ME	THEM	ME	THEM

❤ SUMMARY OF THE DATE

What where the highlights of the date?

Things you have in common with them?

What do you like about them?

Things that concerns/worries you about them?

Overall feeling of the date?

Would you see them again?

DATE: DATE'S NAME:

WHEN: EXCITEMENT LEVEL:

WHERE:

What do you want out of the date?

....

....

....

....

What do you want to know about them?

....

....

....

....

What do you want them to know about you?

....

....

....

....

Date Fun Silliness Checklist

BATHROOM BREAK COUNT		DRINKS COUNT		TIMES CHECKED PHONE COUNT	
ME	THEM	ME	THEM	ME	THEM

 SUMMARY OF THE DATE

What where the highlights of the date?

Things you have in common with them?

What do you like about them?

Things that concerns/worries you about them?

Overall feeling of the date?

Would you see them again?

DATE:

DATE'S NAME:

WHEN:

EXCITEMENT LEVEL:

WHERE:

What do you want out of the date?

What do you want to know about them?

What do you want them to know about you?

Date Fun Silliness Checklist

BATHROOM BREAK COUNT		DRINKS COUNT		TIMES CHECKED PHONE COUNT	
ME	THEM	ME	THEM	ME	THEM

♥ SUMMARY 🔥F THE DATE

What where the highlights of the date?

Things you have in common with them?

What do you like about them?

Things that concerns/worries you about them?

Overall feeling of the date?

Would you see them again?

DATE:　　　　　　　　DATE'S NAME:

WHEN:　　　　　　　　EXCITEMENT LEVEL:

WHERE:

What do you want out of the date?

What do you want to know about them?

What do you want them to know about you?

Date Fun Silliness Checklist

BATHROOM BREAK COUNT		DRINKS COUNT		TIMES CHECKED PHONE COUNT	
ME	THEM	ME	THEM	ME	THEM

❤ SUMMARY 🔥F THE DATE

What where the highlights of the date?

Things you have in common with them?

What do you like about them?

Things that concerns/worries you about them?

Overall feeling of the date?

Would you see them again?

DATE: DATE'S NAME:

WHEN: EXCITEMENT LEVEL:

WHERE:

What do you want out of the date?

What do you want to know about them?

What do you want them to know about you?

Date Fun Silliness Checklist

BATHROOM BREAK COUNT		DRINKS COUNT		TIMES CHECKED PHONE COUNT	
ME	THEM	ME	THEM	ME	THEM

♥ SUMMARY 🔥F THE DATE

What where the highlights of the date?

Things you have in common with them?

What do you like about them?

Things that concerns/worries you about them?

Overall feeling of the date?

Would you see them again?

DATE: **DATE'S NAME:**

WHEN: **EXCITEMENT LEVEL:**

WHERE:

What do you want out of the date?

What do you want to know about them?

What do you want them to know about you?

🥂🎳🎉 :-: **Date Fun Silliness Checklist** :-: 🎉🎳🥂

BATHROOM BREAK COUNT		DRINKS COUNT		TIMES CHECKED PHONE COUNT	
ME	THEM	ME	THEM	ME	THEM

💔 SUMMARY 🔥F THE DATE

What where the highlights of the date?

Things you have in common with them?

What do you like about them?

Things that concerns/worries you about them?

Overall feeling of the date?

Would you see them again?

DATE: DATE'S NAME:

WHEN: EXCITEMENT LEVEL: ♡▱▱♡

WHERE:

What do you want out of the date?

....
....
....

What do you want to know about them?

....
....
....

What do you want them to know about you?

....
....
....

🥂🎳💐 :-: **Date Fun Silliness Checklist** :-: 💐🎳🥂

BATHROOM BREAK COUNT		DRINKS COUNT		TIMES CHECKED PHONE COUNT	
ME	THEM	ME	THEM	ME	THEM

♥ SUMMARY  OF THE DATE

What where the highlights of the date?

Things you have in common with them?

What do you like about them?

Things that concerns/worries you about them?

Overall feeling of the date?

Would you see them again?

DATE:

DATE'S NAME:

WHEN:

EXCITEMENT LEVEL:

WHERE:

What do you want out of the date?

What do you want to know about them?

What do you want them to know about you?

Date Fun Silliness Checklist

BATHROOM BREAK COUNT		DRINKS COUNT		TIMES CHECKED PHONE COUNT	
ME	THEM	ME	THEM	ME	THEM

♥ SUMMARY 🔥F THE DATE

What where the highlights of the date?

Things you have in common with them?

What do you like about them?

Things that concerns/worries you about them?

Overall feeling of the date?

Would you see them again?

DATE: DATE'S NAME:

WHEN: EXCITEMENT LEVEL: ♡▱♡

WHERE:

What do you want out of the date?

What do you want to know about them?

What do you want them to know about you?

Date Fun Silliness Checklist

BATHROOM BREAK COUNT		DRINKS COUNT		TIMES CHECKED PHONE COUNT	
ME	THEM	ME	THEM	ME	THEM

💔 SUMMARY 🔥F THE DATE

What where the highlights of the date?

Things you have in common with them?

What do you like about them?

Things that concerns/worries you about them?

Overall feeling of the date?

Would you see them again?

DATE: DATE'S NAME:

WHEN: EXCITEMENT LEVEL:

WHERE:

What do you want out of the date?

What do you want to know about them?

What do you want them to know about you?

Date Fun Silliness Checklist

BATHROOM BREAK COUNT		DRINKS COUNT		TIMES CHECKED PHONE COUNT	
ME	THEM	ME	THEM	ME	THEM

 SUMMARY OF THE DATE

What where the highlights of the date?

Things you have in common with them?

What do you like about them?

Things that concerns/worries you about them?

Overall feeling of the date?

Would you see them again?

DATE: DATE'S NAME:

WHEN: EXCITEMENT LEVEL:

WHERE:

What do you want out of the date?

....

....

....

....

What do you want to know about them?

....

....

....

....

What do you want them to know about you?

....

....

....

....

Date Fun Silliness Checklist

BATHROOM BREAK COUNT		DRINKS COUNT		TIMES CHECKED PHONE COUNT	
ME	THEM	ME	THEM	ME	THEM

 SUMMARY OF THE DATE

What where the highlights of the date?

Things you have in common with them?

What do you like about them?

Things that concerns/worries you about them?

Overall feeling of the date?

Would you see them again?

DATE:

DATE'S NAME:

WHEN:

EXCITEMENT LEVEL:

WHERE:

What do you want out of the date?

What do you want to know about them?

What do you want them to know about you?

Date Fun Silliness Checklist

BATHROOM BREAK COUNT		DRINKS COUNT		TIMES CHECKED PHONE COUNT	
ME	THEM	ME	THEM	ME	THEM

💔 SUMMARY 🔥F THE DATE

What where the highlights of the date?

Things you have in common with them?

What do you like about them?

Things that concerns/worries you about them?

Overall feeling of the date?

Would you see them again?

DATE:

DATE'S NAME:

WHEN:

EXCITEMENT LEVEL:

WHERE:

What do you want out of the date?

What do you want to know about them?

What do you want them to know about you?

Date Fun Silliness Checklist

BATHROOM BREAK COUNT		DRINKS COUNT		TIMES CHECKED PHONE COUNT	
ME	THEM	ME	THEM	ME	THEM

💔 SUMMARY F THE DATE

What where the highlights of the date?

Things you have in common with them?

What do you like about them?

Things that concerns/worries you about them?

Overall feeling of the date?

Would you see them again?

DATE:

DATE'S NAME:

WHEN:

EXCITEMENT LEVEL:

WHERE:

What do you want out of the date?

What do you want to know about them?

What do you want them to know about you?

Date Fun Silliness Checklist

BATHROOM BREAK COUNT		DRINKS COUNT		TIMES CHECKED PHONE COUNT	
ME	THEM	ME	THEM	ME	THEM

 SUMMARY OF THE DATE

What where the highlights of the date?

Things you have in common with them?

What do you like about them?

Things that concerns/worries you about them?

Overall feeling of the date?

Would you see them again?

DATE:

DATE'S NAME:

WHEN:

EXCITEMENT LEVEL:

WHERE:

What do you want out of the date?

What do you want to know about them?

What do you want them to know about you?

Date Fun Silliness Checklist

BATHROOM BREAK COUNT		DRINKS COUNT		TIMES CHECKED PHONE COUNT	
ME	THEM	ME	THEM	ME	THEM

♥ SUMMARY F THE DATE

What where the highlights of the date?

Things you have in common with them?

What do you like about them?

Things that concerns/worries you about them?

Overall feeling of the date?

Would you see them again?

DATE:

DATE'S NAME:

WHEN:

EXCITEMENT LEVEL:

WHERE:

What do you want out of the date?

What do you want to know about them?

What do you want them to know about you?

Date Fun Silliness Checklist

BATHROOM BREAK COUNT		DRINKS COUNT		TIMES CHECKED PHONE COUNT	
ME	THEM	ME	THEM	ME	THEM

💔 SUMMARY 🔥F THE DATE

What where the highlights of the date?

Things you have in common with them?

What do you like about them?

Things that concerns/worries you about them?

Overall feeling of the date?

Would you see them again?

DATE:

DATE'S NAME:

WHEN:

EXCITEMENT LEVEL:

WHERE:

What do you want out of the date?

What do you want to know about them?

What do you want them to know about you?

Date Fun Silliness Checklist

BATHROOM BREAK COUNT		DRINKS COUNT		TIMES CHECKED PHONE COUNT	
ME	THEM	ME	THEM	ME	THEM

♥ SUMMARY F THE DATE

What where the highlights of the date?

Things you have in common with them?

What do you like about them?

Things that concerns/worries you about them?

Overall feeling of the date?

Would you see them again?

DATE:

DATE'S NAME:

WHEN:

EXCITEMENT LEVEL:

WHERE:

What do you want out of the date?

What do you want to know about them?

What do you want them to know about you?

Date Fun Silliness Checklist

BATHROOM BREAK COUNT		DRINKS COUNT		TIMES CHECKED PHONE COUNT	
ME	THEM	ME	THEM	ME	THEM

 SUMMARY OF THE DATE

What where the highlights of the date?

Things you have in common with them?

What do you like about them?

Things that concerns/worries you about them?

Overall feeling of the date?

Would you see them again?

DATE:

DATE'S NAME:

WHEN:

EXCITEMENT LEVEL:

WHERE:

What do you want out of the date?

What do you want to know about them?

What do you want them to know about you?

Date Fun Silliness Checklist

BATHROOM BREAK COUNT		DRINKS COUNT		TIMES CHECKED PHONE COUNT	
ME	THEM	ME	THEM	ME	THEM

 SUMMARY OF THE DATE

What where the highlights of the date?

Things you have in common with them?

What do you like about them?

Things that concerns/worries you about them?

Overall feeling of the date?

Would you see them again?

DATE:

DATE'S NAME:

WHEN:

EXCITEMENT LEVEL:

WHERE:

What do you want out of the date?

What do you want to know about them?

What do you want them to know about you?

Date Fun Silliness Checklist

BATHROOM BREAK COUNT		DRINKS COUNT		TIMES CHECKED PHONE COUNT	
ME	THEM	ME	THEM	ME	THEM

 SUMMARY OF THE DATE

What where the highlights of the date?

Things you have in common with them?

What do you like about them?

Things that concerns/worries you about them?

Overall feeling of the date?

Would you see them again?

DATE:

DATE'S NAME:

WHEN:

EXCITEMENT LEVEL:

WHERE:

What do you want out of the date?

What do you want to know about them?

What do you want them to know about you?

Date Fun Silliness Checklist

BATHROOM BREAK COUNT		DRINKS COUNT		TIMES CHECKED PHONE COUNT	
ME	THEM	ME	THEM	ME	THEM

♥ SUMMARY F THE DATE

What where the highlights of the date?

Things you have in common with them?

What do you like about them?

Things that concerns/worries you about them?

Overall feeling of the date?

Would you see them again?

DATE:

DATE'S NAME:

WHEN:

EXCITEMENT LEVEL:

WHERE:

What do you want out of the date?

What do you want to know about them?

What do you want them to know about you?

Date Fun Silliness Checklist

BATHROOM BREAK COUNT		DRINKS COUNT		TIMES CHECKED PHONE COUNT	
ME	THEM	ME	THEM	ME	THEM

 SUMMARY OF THE DATE

What where the highlights of the date?

Things you have in common with them?

What do you like about them?

Things that concerns/worries you about them?

Overall feeling of the date?

Would you see them again?

DATE:

DATE'S NAME:

WHEN:

EXCITEMENT LEVEL:

WHERE:

What do you want out of the date?

What do you want to know about them?

What do you want them to know about you?

Date Fun Silliness Checklist

BATHROOM BREAK COUNT		DRINKS COUNT		TIMES CHECKED PHONE COUNT	
ME	THEM	ME	THEM	ME	THEM

💔 SUMMARY  THE DATE

What where the highlights of the date?

Things you have in common with them?

What do you like about them?

Things that concerns/worries you about them?

Overall feeling of the date?

Would you see them again?

DATE:

DATE'S NAME:

WHEN:

EXCITEMENT LEVEL:

WHERE:

What do you want out of the date?

What do you want to know about them?

What do you want them to know about you?

Date Fun Silliness Checklist

BATHROOM BREAK COUNT		DRINKS COUNT		TIMES CHECKED PHONE COUNT	
ME	THEM	ME	THEM	ME	THEM

♥ SUMMARY F THE DATE

What where the highlights of the date?

Things you have in common with them?

What do you like about them?

Things that concerns/worries you about them?

Overall feeling of the date?

Would you see them again?

DATE:

DATE'S NAME:

WHEN:

EXCITEMENT LEVEL:

WHERE:

What do you want out of the date?

What do you want to know about them?

What do you want them to know about you?

Date Fun Silliness Checklist

BATHROOM BREAK COUNT		DRINKS COUNT		TIMES CHECKED PHONE COUNT	
ME	THEM	ME	THEM	ME	THEM

💔 SUMMARY 🔥F THE DATE

What where the highlights of the date?

Things you have in common with them?

What do you like about them?

Things that concerns/worries you about them?

Overall feeling of the date?

Would you see them again?

DATE:

DATE'S NAME:

WHEN:

EXCITEMENT LEVEL:

WHERE:

What do you want out of the date?

What do you want to know about them?

What do you want them to know about you?

Date Fun Silliness Checklist

BATHROOM BREAK COUNT		DRINKS COUNT		TIMES CHECKED PHONE COUNT	
ME	THEM	ME	THEM	ME	THEM

SUMMARY OF THE DATE

What where the highlights of the date?

Things you have in common with them?

What do you like about them?

Things that concerns/worries you about them?

Overall feeling of the date?

Would you see them again?

DATE:

DATE'S NAME:

WHEN:

EXCITEMENT LEVEL:

WHERE:

What do you want out of the date?

What do you want to know about them?

What do you want them to know about you?

Date Fun Silliness Checklist

BATHROOM BREAK COUNT		DRINKS COUNT		TIMES CHECKED PHONE COUNT	
ME	THEM	ME	THEM	ME	THEM

♥ SUMMARY F THE DATE

What where the highlights of the date?

Things you have in common with them?

What do you like about them?

Things that concerns/worries you about them?

Overall feeling of the date?

Would you see them again?

DATE:

DATE'S NAME:

WHEN:

EXCITEMENT LEVEL:

WHERE:

What do you want out of the date?

What do you want to know about them?

What do you want them to know about you?

🥂🎳💐 :-) **Date Fun Silliness Checklist** :-(💐🎳🥂

BATHROOM BREAK COUNT		DRINKS COUNT		TIMES CHECKED PHONE COUNT	
ME	THEM	ME	THEM	ME	THEM

 SUMMARY OF THE DATE

What where the highlights of the date?

Things you have in common with them?

What do you like about them?

Things that concerns/worries you about them?

Overall feeling of the date?

Would you see them again?

DATE:

DATE'S NAME:

WHEN:

EXCITEMENT LEVEL:

WHERE:

What do you want out of the date?

What do you want to know about them?

What do you want them to know about you?

Date Fun Silliness Checklist

BATHROOM BREAK COUNT		DRINKS COUNT		TIMES CHECKED PHONE COUNT	
ME	THEM	ME	THEM	ME	THEM

 SUMMARY OF THE DATE

What where the highlights of the date?

Things you have in common with them?

What do you like about them?

Things that concerns/worries you about them?

Overall feeling of the date?

Would you see them again?

DATE:

DATE'S NAME:

WHEN:

EXCITEMENT LEVEL:

WHERE:

What do you want out of the date?

What do you want to know about them?

What do you want them to know about you?

Date Fun Silliness Checklist

BATHROOM BREAK COUNT		DRINKS COUNT		TIMES CHECKED PHONE COUNT	
ME	THEM	ME	THEM	ME	THEM

💔 SUMMARY F THE DATE

What where the highlights of the date?

Things you have in common with them?

What do you like about them?

Things that concerns/worries you about them?

Overall feeling of the date?

Would you see them again?

DATE:

DATE'S NAME:

WHEN:

EXCITEMENT LEVEL:

WHERE:

What do you want out of the date?

What do you want to know about them?

What do you want them to know about you?

Date Fun Silliness Checklist

BATHROOM BREAK COUNT		DRINKS COUNT		TIMES CHECKED PHONE COUNT	
ME	THEM	ME	THEM	ME	THEM

💔 SUMMARY 🔥F THE DATE

What where the highlights of the date?

Things you have in common with them?

What do you like about them?

Things that concerns/worries you about them?

Overall feeling of the date?

Would you see them again?

DATE:

DATE'S NAME:

WHEN:

EXCITEMENT LEVEL:

WHERE:

What do you want out of the date?

What do you want to know about them?

What do you want them to know about you?

Date Fun Silliness Checklist

BATHROOM BREAK COUNT		DRINKS COUNT		TIMES CHECKED PHONE COUNT	
ME	THEM	ME	THEM	ME	THEM

♥ SUMMARY F THE DATE

What where the highlights of the date?

Things you have in common with them?

What do you like about them?

Things that concerns/worries you about them?

Overall feeling of the date?

Would you see them again?

DATE:

DATE'S NAME:

WHEN:

EXCITEMENT LEVEL:

WHERE:

What do you want out of the date?

What do you want to know about them?

What do you want them to know about you?

Date Fun Silliness Checklist

BATHROOM BREAK COUNT		DRINKS COUNT		TIMES CHECKED PHONE COUNT	
ME	THEM	ME	THEM	ME	THEM

 SUMMARY OF THE DATE

What where the highlights of the date?

Things you have in common with them?

What do you like about them?

Things that concerns/worries you about them?

Overall feeling of the date?

Would you see them again?

DATE:

DATE'S NAME:

WHEN:

EXCITEMENT LEVEL:

WHERE:

What do you want out of the date?

What do you want to know about them?

What do you want them to know about you?

Date Fun Silliness Checklist

BATHROOM BREAK COUNT		DRINKS COUNT		TIMES CHECKED PHONE COUNT	
ME	THEM	ME	THEM	ME	THEM

 SUMMARY OF THE DATE

What where the highlights of the date?

Things you have in common with them?

What do you like about them?

Things that concerns/worries you about them?

Overall feeling of the date?

Would you see them again?

DATE:

DATE'S NAME:

WHEN:

EXCITEMENT LEVEL:

WHERE:

What do you want out of the date?

What do you want to know about them?

What do you want them to know about you?

Date Fun Silliness Checklist

BATHROOM BREAK COUNT		DRINKS COUNT		TIMES CHECKED PHONE COUNT	
ME	THEM	ME	THEM	ME	THEM

 SUMMARY OF THE DATE

What where the highlights of the date?

Things you have in common with them?

What do you like about them?

Things that concerns/worries you about them?

Overall feeling of the date?

Would you see them again?

DATE:

DATE'S NAME:

WHEN:

EXCITEMENT LEVEL:

WHERE:

What do you want out of the date?

What do you want to know about them?

What do you want them to know about you?

Date Fun Silliness Checklist

BATHROOM BREAK COUNT		DRINKS COUNT		TIMES CHECKED PHONE COUNT	
ME	THEM	ME	THEM	ME	THEM

 SUMMARY OF THE DATE

What where the highlights of the date?

Things you have in common with them?

What do you like about them?

Things that concerns/worries you about them?

Overall feeling of the date?

Would you see them again?

DATE:

DATE'S NAME:

WHEN:

EXCITEMENT LEVEL:

WHERE:

What do you want out of the date?

What do you want to know about them?

What do you want them to know about you?

Date Fun Silliness Checklist

BATHROOM BREAK COUNT		DRINKS COUNT		TIMES CHECKED PHONE COUNT	
ME	THEM	ME	THEM	ME	THEM

💔 SUMMARY 🔥F THE DATE

What where the highlights of the date?

Things you have in common with them?

What do you like about them?

Things that concerns/worries you about them?

Overall feeling of the date?

Would you see them again?

Printed in Great Britain
by Amazon